Decadent

Gluten-free Treats

First published in 2013 by New Holland Publishers (NZ) Ltd
Auckland · Sydney · London · Cape Town

www.newhollandpublishers.co.nz

218 Lake Road, Northcote, Auckland 0627, New Zealand
Unit 1, 66 Gibbes Street, Chatswood, NSW 2067, Australia
86–88 Edgware Road, London W2 2EA, United Kingdom
Wembley Square, First Floor, Solan Road, Gardens, Cape Town 8001, South Africa

Publishing manager: Christine Thomson
Editor: Sarah Elworthy
Design and illustration: Rachel Kirkland at The Fount
Photography: Devin Hart

National Library of New Zealand Cataloguing-in-Publication Data

Jane, Tamara.
Decadent gluten-free treats : with tempting vegan & dairy-free
options / Tamara Jane ; photography by Devin Hart.
Includes index.
ISBN 978-8-86966-393-3
1. Gluten-free diet—Recipes. 2. Baking. I. Hart, Devin. II. Title.
641.56318—dc 23

10 9 8 7 6 5 4 3 2 1

Colour reproduction by Image Centre, Auckland
Printed in China by Toppan Leefung Printing Ltd, on paper sourced from sustainable forests.

Decadent
Gluten-free Treats

With tempting vegan & dairy-free options

TAMARA JANE
Photography by Devin Hart

NEW HOLLAND

Contents

Cookies, Slices and Scones

Cupcakes

Cakes

86

Frostings and Toppings

100

Introduction

Welcome to book number three, and a very special one for anyone who suffers from allergies, dietary restrictions or has chosen to follow a special diet.

I am passionate about baking, and feel that people who cannot enjoy the pleasure of a freshly baked scone, or a piece of a workmate's birthday cake are overlooked in this area. I have developed an intolerance to gluten over my years of baking, but in the past have chosen not to eat the gluten free options on offer as they were often pasty, unappetising or just didn't taste good. Many of the recipes in this book are ones I make for family and friends again and again, and most people don't even realise that the treat they are enjoying is in fact gluten free.

While most of the recipes in this book are gluten free we have included some decadent treats for those who cannot eat eggs, dairy or a combination of the two. We know that you all need to indulge in a little sweet treat and hope these recipes will give you pleasure on that special occasion. Be sure to check the key symbols on each recipe, coded for quick reference, as follows:

GF – Gluten free   EF – Egg free

DF – Dairy free   V – Vegan

While researching for new and additional recipe ideas, I came across many baked items that were already wheat, egg or dairy free. Macaroons, meringues, friands and some biscuits already in your repertoire will need no adjustment. Just take a careful look at the ingredients list to make sure everything is gluten free.

There are some weird and wonderful replacements for flours and eggs that will recreate the light and fluffy structure of a cake, or the tender crumb of a biscuit. Most are readily available from health-food stores, organic shops or a well-stocked supermarket. Some you may have to look for online, and search for a supplier close to you. Unfortunately, when baking with specialty ingredients, the one unavoidable thing is the cost involved. However, it is worth it when baking a cake for a child with a severe egg allergy who can then eat their birthday cake for the first time — seeing that look of pleasure is something I get a thrill out of every time.

We have photographed this book to show you how that finished product should look, no trickery, no super magical skills required. I feel that you will be able to achieve the same results we have by using the 'how to's' and a bit of piping practice. A palette knife will become easier to use with each cake you ice and decorate.

Tamara Jane

The Right Ingredients

Gluten-free baking basics are now readily available in most supermarkets. Gluten-free premixed flours (plain and self raising) are a good place to begin, as they remove the difficulty of measuring different types of starches.

When using your pantry staples, always read the labels to make sure they are gluten free. Cocoa, baking powder, icing sugar and cornflour are all available gluten free.

Amaranth Flour

Amaranth flour is very high in protein, fibre and lysine, an essential amino acid. It has a pleasant, nutty taste and combines well with other flours in gluten-free baked goods. Use it as a proportion, about 15%, of total flour ratio, in gluten-free baking mixes to increase the protein content of baked goods.

Buckwheat Flour

Buckwheat is a seed related to rhubarb, and is one of the best sources of high quality protein in the plant kingdom as it is easily digested and is high in minerals. It also has a balanced amino acid profile. Buckwheat is high in potassium, phosphorus and has more vitamin B than wheat. Ground into flour its nutty taste enhances the texture of muffins and pancakes.

Butter

Unsalted butter is my choice in baking as it doesn't alter the flavour of the final item. In frostings it is essential.

Have butter at room temperature when you begin. If the butter is too cold it may be microwaved on low power until just soft, but make sure you don't melt it.

Chocolate

Dark chocolate (at least 72% cocoa) contains no dairy products (although it will not necessarily be vegan — read the labels carefully when buying). I have used 72% chocolate in all the dairy-free recipes containing dark chocolate. Non-dairy white chocolate bars and milk chocolate chips are available from good health and organic shops.

Cocoa Powder

I always use a non-alkaline Dutch process cocoa powder, as it has a much more intense chocolate flavour and no fillers. If the cocoa is lumpy you will need to sift it first.

Coconut Flour

Coconut flour can be used in small quantities in gluten free recipes to increase the fibre content. Coconut flour is almost 60% fibre and is lower in carbohydrates than other gluten-free flours. Coconut flour works best in recipes that include eggs and has a short shelf life, so refrigerate baked goods made with coconut flour to prevent spoilage.

Coconut Sugar

Coconut sugar has gained popularity as a health food, especially among people with diabetes. It is derived from the sap of the flower buds of the coconut palm and can be used as a sugar substitute. Because it is naturally low on the Glycemic Index, it is considered safe to use for diabetics. It has a brown sugar, almost caramel flavour and can be used interchangeably with other sugars.

Eggs

I always use large eggs (about 65g or size 7). Whether or not you use free-range eggs is your choice.

Eggs are best at room temperature to allow for easy blending into the mixture. To bring eggs to room temperature quickly, you can place them in a bowl of warm water for about 10 minutes.

Ground Almonds

(Almond Meal or Almond Flour)

Ground almonds are high in fibre and mono-unsaturated fat, and will add moisture, flavour, texture and nutritional value to gluten-free baked goods. Nut flours, including almond, pecan or hazelnut, also make delicious coatings for chicken, fish or vegetables. Nut flours can also be used to replace powdered milk in most recipes, making them a useful, dairy-free alternative ingredient.

Ground Flaxseed

(Flaxseed Meal)

Made from ground flaxseeds (linseeds), this is high in omega-3 and vitamin B and very high in fibre. Ground flaxseed meal goes rancid quite quickly, so to extend its shelf life store it in an airtight container in the refrigerator. When mixed with water the ground flaxseed becomes mucilaginous like egg white, so makes an excellent egg substitute in vegan baking. Golden or brown ground flaxseed can be used interchangeably.

Guar Gum

Guar gum comes from the seed of bean-like plant, sometimes referred to as the Indian tree. It is high in soluble fibre and is used as a stabiliser and thickener in the commercial food industry. Measure carefully when using guar gum or you may end up with heavy, stringy baked goods. Guar gum adds structure and hold to gluten-free baked items.

Milk Alternatives

When baking for vegans there are many options available as milk replacements in recipes. I have successfully used soy, rice and almond milks. Which milk you choose comes down to taste, fat and nutrition content and any other allergies.

Non-dairy Spreads

There are multiple brands and types of dairy-free spreads readily available. Nuttelex, olive oil-based spreads, soy spreads and nut butters can all be used in vegan and dairy-free baking. Sometimes the moisture content is higher than butter so check the consistency before adding the full amount of liquid to a mixture.

Potato Flour

Potato flour is made from peeled and cooked potato which is mashed, dried and ground, and mixed with ground whole potato flakes. Often used as a thickener.

Potato Starch

Potato starch is a refined starch used to add moisture and texture. Add to gluten-free flour mixes and recipes for light, fine-textured baked goods. Like other starches, including cornflour, arrowroot and tapioca, potato is high in refined carbohydrates and low in fibre and nutrients.

Quinoa Flour

Quinoa is a protein-rich grain, and was a major food source for the ancient Incas. Quinoa is available as whole seed, flakes and flour. Quinoa flour has a somewhat strong, bitter flavour, but can be used in small amounts in gluten-free mixes and baking recipes to improve nutritional quality.

Raising Agents

Baking soda and baking powder are not interchangeable and must be used in the amount specified. Too little or too much will result in dramatically different results, so read and measure carefully. Check your baking powder label to make sure it's gluten free.

Rice Flour

White rice flour and sweet rice flour add lightness and texture to gluten-free baked goods. Use rice flours in combination with other gluten-free flours for better texture and nutritional quality. Small amounts of sweet rice flour will improve the texture and 'chew' of gluten-free baked goods, and works as a thickener in sauce recipes and is used to dust baking pans to prevent sticking.

Soy Flour

Soy flour is naturally high in protein and fats but it is available as a processed and low-fat product. It adds moisture and texture to baked goods and browns quickly.

Tapioca Flour

(Tapioca Starch)

Tapioca flour is ground from the root of the tropical cassava plant, used extensively in commercial gluten-free products. It is a flavourless, high-carbohydrate starch that is very low in nutrients. Use it as a proportion, up to 50%, of total flour ratio, in gluten-free baking mixes to lighten the texture of baked goods. It can also be used in batters and crumb recipes for crisp, golden crusts.

Vanilla and Flavours

Flavourings are so important to the final product, so use the best quality you can afford. Vanilla bean extract or essence is far superior in flavour to artificial essence.

Xanthan Gum

Xanthan gum is a corn-based, fermented product. It is used extensively in the food industry as a thickener and is a common ingredient in gluten free recipes. Make sure you measure xantham gum carefully when using, as too much may result in a heavy, gummy or even 'slimy' texture in your baked goods.

Tools and Equipment

Cake-making supplies are easily sourced from good homeware stores, the supermarket and the multitude of online suppliers. There are specialty cake-decoration shops to browse online, and I love to scan the internet for the newest and most innovative tools.

Baking Paper

Use silicon or greaseproof paper, not the waxed kind. This is essential when making slices baked with sticky, caramel-based toppings, and makes cleaning the pans and trays much easier.

Cupcake Papers

These are available from supermarkets in a range of sizes and colours.

Flower Cutters, Moulds and Cookie Cutters

Flower cutters, silicon moulds, florists' wire, piping bags and nozzles and chocolate transfer sheets can be purchased from speciality cake-decoration suppliers. Cutters are available from homeware stores in a range of sizes and shapes and are ideal for making gingerbread shapes and chocolate cut-outs. The best place to source small speciality items is the internet — there are many suppliers online with hundreds of items to choose from.

Kitchen Scales

When working with delicate recipes, such as macaroons, electronic scales make the job of weighing ingredients much easier. They don't have to be expensive, but any scales that have small size increments, such as 1–5g, are more accurate.

Mixers

A set of hand-held electric beaters will make the job of mixing cakes easier. A stand mixer, such as a KitchenAid is a good investment if you intend to make a lot of cakes, but is not essential. The only mixture that absolutely requires a stand mixer is the flower paste, as it's a very stiff paste and will burn out the motor of your hand-held beater.

Mixing Bowls

A selection of sizes is important with good sturdy weight to stop the bowl slipping when using the mixer. A ceramic or glass bowl is useful as you can put this into the microwave to soften butter and make ganache.

Muffin Trays

These are available from most supermarkets and homeware suppliers, and come in a range of sizes.

The recipes in this book are all made using a standard 12-hole muffin tray. If you use a different-sized tray be aware this will change the number of cakes you make and the time the cakes take to bake.

Non-stick Mats and Rolling Pins

These are available from cake-decoration suppliers. They make the job of rolling flower paste much easier, enabling you to roll a much thinner paste. A silicon mat to cover the paste on the board will stop it from drying out while you create your decorations.

Slice and Cake Pans

When making larger cakes, line the base and sides of the pan with baking paper before filling with the cake batter. This will make the removal of the cake and the cleaning of the pan much easier. The size of your pan compared to the recipe will have an impact on the baking time for your cake.

Small Utensils

Measuring cups, spoons, jugs and scales are available from homeware stores. Palette knives, small rolling pins and rubber template mats can be purchased from cake-decoration suppliers.

Cookies, Slices and Scones

Double Chocolate and Raspberry Cookies

MAKES 24

125g butter

1 cup brown sugar

1 egg

¾ cup tapioca flour

½ cup rice flour

1 teaspoon gluten-free baking powder

¼ cup cocoa

30g freeze-dried raspberries, crushed

100g white chocolate chips

{ GF }

Preheat the oven to 180°C. Line two baking trays with baking paper.

Soften the butter and place in a bowl with the brown sugar and the egg. Using electric beaters, beat together until light and creamy.

Stir in the sifted flours, baking powder and cocoa, then add the raspberries and white chocolate chips. Mix until well combined, ensuring there are no lumps of flour in the mixture.

Use a spoon to place heaped mounds onto the prepared trays. Leave about 5cm between each cookie to allow for spreading.

Bake for about 15 minutes, until the edges are beginning to turn a darker brown. This can be difficult to judge, but you will see a distinct dark rim appear around the edge.

Allow to cool on the tray.

Store in an airtight container.

Chocolate Chip and Smarties Cookies

MAKES 18

250g butter

¾ cup caster sugar

200g condensed milk

2½ cups gluten-free
self-raising flour

1 teaspoon guar gum

1 teaspoon vanilla extract
or essence

100g chocolate chips

200g Smarties

{ GF EF }

Preheat the oven to 180°C. Line three baking trays with baking paper.

Using electric beaters, cream the butter, sugar and condensed milk until light and smooth.

Stir in the sifted flour, guar gum and vanilla, then add the chocolate chips and Smarties. Stir until well combined.

Roll tablespoonfuls of the mixture into balls and place on the prepared trays. Flatten slightly. Allow room for spreading between each cookie.

Bake for about 15 minutes or until golden brown.

Allow to cool on the tray for 5 minutes before removing to a wire rack to cool completely.

Store in an airtight container.

Coffee Shortbread

MAKES 24

250g butter, softened

1 cup gluten-free icing sugar

3 teaspoons instant coffee powder

3 teaspoons cold water

2¾ cups gluten-free plain flour

demerara or white sugar, to sprinkle

{ GF EF }

Preheat the oven to 180°C. Line a baking tray with baking paper.

Place the softened butter and icing sugar into a bowl and using electric beaters, mix until light and creamy.

In a small cup, dissolve the coffee powder in the water. Beat into the creamed mixture.

Add in the flour and using your hands, bring the mixture together into a firm dough.

Take tablespoons of the dough and roll into walnut-sized balls. Place these on the prepared tray.

Press the top of each ball with a fork to indent and sprinkle with a little sugar.

Bake for 15 minutes until pale brown in colour.

Allow to cool on the tray for 5 minutes before removing to a wire rack to cool completely.

Store in an airtight container.

Peanut Butter Cookies

MAKES 24

1 cup white sugar

1 cup crunchy peanut butter

1 egg

1 teaspoon baking soda

{ GF DF }

Preheat the oven to 180°C. Line two baking trays with baking paper.

Combine the sugar and peanut butter in a bowl, and stir until smooth. Mix in the egg and baking soda and stir until well combined.

Roll teaspoonfuls of the mixture into balls and place on the prepared trays. Leave at least 3cm between each cookie to allow for spreading.

Bake for about 10 minutes, until golden brown.

Allow to cool on the tray for 5 minutes before removing to a wire rack to cool completely.

Store in an airtight container.

Lemon Shortbread Rounds

MAKES ABOUT 18

180g non-dairy spread

¾ cup coconut sugar

1 teaspoon vanilla extract or essence

2 teaspoons finely grated lemon zest

1¼ cups rice flour, sifted

¼ cup tapioca flour, sifted

½ cup gluten-free cornflour, sifted

⅛ teaspoon gluten-free baking powder

pinch of salt

{ GF DF EF V }

Preheat the oven to 180°C. Grease and line a 20cm x 30cm slice pan with baking paper.

Place the spread, coconut sugar, vanilla and zest into a bowl and using electric beaters, cream until well combined.

Stir in the sifted dry ingredients and beat on a low speed until a soft dough is formed.

Remove from the bowl and tip dough onto a sheet of baking paper lightly dusted with cornflour. Cover with another sheet of baking paper and roll the dough out between the two sheets.

Using a 5cm cutter, press out rounds of dough and place on a baking tray.

Bake for about 15 minutes until light golden brown.

Remove cookies onto a rack and allow to cool completely.

Store in an airtight container.

Chocolate Whoopie Pies

MAKES 10 FILLED COOKIES

125g butter

1 cup caster sugar

½ teaspoon vanilla extract or essence

2 eggs

¾ cup rice flour

¼ cup potato flour

½ cup gluten-free cornflour

½ cup cocoa

½ teaspoon gluten-free baking powder

1½ teaspoons baking soda

1 teaspoon guar gum

⅓ cup milk

2 tablespoons sour cream

Chocolate Frosting (see page 103) or Dark Chocolate Ganache (see page 106)

{ GF }

Preheat the oven to 200°C. Line three baking trays with baking paper.

Using electric beaters, cream the butter, sugar and vanilla until light and fluffy. Add the eggs one at a time, beating well after each addition.

Add the sifted flours, cocoa, baking powder, baking soda and guar gum.

In a separate small bowl or jug, mix together the milk and sour cream. Add to the mixture and stir together until just combined. The mixture should be a soft dropping consistency.

Fill a piping bag fitted with a 1cm plain round nozzle with the batter.

Pipe small rounds about 3cm in diameter onto the prepared trays. Leave 5cm between each to allow for spreading.

Bake for about 10 minutes or until firm to the touch.

Allow to cool on the trays.

Once cool, ice with Chocolate Frosting or sandwich pairs together using Dark Chocolate Ganache.

Store in an airtight container in the refrigerator.

Coconut and Apricot Macaroons

MAKES 25 MACAROONS

3 cups shredded coconut

4 egg whites

¼ teaspoon salt

¾ cup caster sugar

2 teaspoons vanilla extract
or essence

½ cup dried apricots,
finely chopped

{ GF DF }

Preheat the oven to 170°C. Line three baking trays with baking paper.

Spread the coconut over two of the trays and cook in the oven, tossing occasionally, for 3–4 minutes or until lightly toasted. Allow to cool completely.

In a large, clean, dry bowl, beat the egg whites and salt together with electric beaters, until soft peaks form. Add the sugar a teaspoonful at a time, beating well after each addition. Beat for a further two minutes or until the mixture is thick and glossy.

Add the vanilla and beat to combine.

Add the toasted coconut and apricots. Use a large metal spoon to fold in until just combined.

Place tablespoonfuls of mixture onto the prepared trays, leaving about 2cm between each.

Bake for 12–15 minutes or until light golden and firm.

Allow to cool on the tray for 5 minutes before removing to a wire rack to cool completely.

Store in an airtight container.

Chocolate Macarons

MAKES 20 FILLED MACARONS

Note: when making macarons it is essential to measure the ingredients accurately. In these two macaron recipes I have given the weights of each ingredient, rather than measures, in order to ensure that the balance of egg white to dry ingredients is spot on.

180g ground almonds

30g cocoa

200g gluten-free icing sugar

75ml water

200g caster sugar

160g egg white

Dark Chocolate Ganache
(see page 106)

 { GF DF }

Preheat the oven to 150°C. Line three baking trays with baking paper.

In a bowl, sift the ground almonds, cocoa and icing sugar through a fine sieve.

In a small saucepan, place the water and caster sugar and bring to the boil. Allow the sugar mixture to reach 115°C without stirring, using a sugar thermometer to gain an accurate reading.

In a separate clean, dry bowl, beat 80g of the egg white with electric beaters, until soft peaks form.

Remove the sugar syrup from the heat and very slowly beat the syrup into the egg white. Continue to beat for about 10 minutes until the mixture is stiff and glossy.

Mix the remaining 80g of egg white into the almond mixture to form a paste.

Stir a little of the beaten egg white mixture into the almond paste to loosen it, then fold through the remaining egg white mixture using a rubber spatula.

Stir the mixture until it falls off the spatula like lava.

Fill a piping bag fitted with a 1cm plain round nozzle with the macaron mixture.

Pipe small dots of the mixture onto the prepared trays, leaving about 3cm between each one.

Leave the trays of macarons on the bench at room temperature until they form crusts. Depending on the weather, this can take from 20 minutes to 1 hour. Touch the top of a macaron and it should not stick to your finger.

Bake for about 15 minutes.

Allow to cool on the trays. Once cool, join pairs together with Dark Chocolate Ganache.

Store in an airtight container in the refrigerator.

Pistachio Macarons

MAKES 20 FILLED MACARONS

200g ground almonds

200g gluten-free icing sugar

75ml water

200g caster sugar

160g egg white

green food colouring

50g pistachio nuts, finely chopped

Pistachio Frosting (see page 102)

GF

Preheat the oven to 150°C. Line three baking trays with baking paper.

In a bowl, sift the ground almonds and icing sugar together through a fine sieve.

In a small saucepan, place the water and caster sugar and bring to the boil. Allow the sugar mixture to reach 115°C without stirring, using a sugar thermometer to gain an accurate reading.

In a separate clean, dry bowl, beat 80g of the egg whites with electric beaters, until soft peaks form.

Remove the sugar syrup from the heat and very slowly beat the syrup into the egg whites. Continue to beat for about 10 minutes until the mixture is stiff and glossy.

Mix the remaining 80g of egg white into the almond mixture to form a paste. Stir in a few drops of green food colouring.

Stir a little of the beaten egg white mixture into the almond paste to loosen it, then fold through the remaining egg white mixture using a rubber spatula.

Stir the mixture until it falls off the spatula like lava.

Fill a piping bag fitted with a 1cm plain round nozzle with the macaron mixture.

Pipe small dots of the mixture onto the prepared trays, leaving about 3cm between each one. Sprinkle each macaron with a little of the chopped pistachio nuts.

Leave the trays of macarons on the bench at room temperature until they form crusts. Depending on the weather, this can take from 20 minutes to 1 hour. Touch the top of a macaron and it should not stick to your finger.

Bake for about 15 minutes.

Allow to cool on the trays. Once cool, join pairs together with Pistachio Frosting.

Store in an airtight container.

Zucchini Chocolate Slice

MAKES 24 PIECES

Base

225g butter

1½ cups sugar

3 eggs

3 teaspoons vanilla extract
   or essence

3 cups gluten-free flour

3 teaspoons gluten-free
   baking powder

Topping

3 cups brown sugar

3 cups desiccated coconut

3 cups chocolate chips

3 eggs

3 cups grated zucchini

{ GF }

Preheat the oven to 180°C. Grease and line a 30cm square cake pan with baking paper.

Cream the butter and sugar together. Add in the eggs one at a time and beat well after each addition.

Stir in the vanilla, sifted flour and baking powder to form a soft dough.

Press into the base of the prepared pan.

Bake for about 15 minutes until golden brown.

While the base is cooking, prepare the topping. Combine all the ingredients together in a bowl. Leave to rest for 10 minutes to thicken a little.

Spread the topping evenly over the hot base and return to the oven for another 30 minutes. The topping should be a light brown colour.

Cool completely in the pan before removing and cutting into squares or fingers.

Store in an airtight container in the refrigerator.

Lemon Slice

MAKES 18 PIECES

Base

1 cup polenta

2 cups ground almonds

½ cup brown or coconut sugar

1 teaspoon finely grated lemon zest

125g butter, softened

1 egg

Topping

1½ cups caster sugar

1 tablespoon finely grated lemon zest

3 eggs

2 tablespoons gluten-free cornflour

2 tablespoons gluten-free custard powder

½ teaspoon gluten-free baking powder

{ GF }

Preheat the oven to 180°C. Grease and line the base and sides of a 24cm square cake pan with baking paper.

To make the base, stir together the polenta, almonds, sugar and zest. Rub in the butter until the mixture is a dry sandy consistency, then add the egg. Keep on mixing until it forms a dough. The dough can also be prepared in a food processor if you prefer.

Press into the base of the prepared pan.

Bake for about 15 minutes until golden brown.

Remove from the oven.

While the base is cooking, prepare the topping. Combine all the topping ingredients together in a bowl and whisk well.

Pour the topping evenly over the hot base and return to the oven for about 30 minutes, or until the topping is set and lightly browned.

Cool completely in the pan before cutting into squares or fingers to serve.

Store in an airtight container in the refrigerator.

Raspberry Lemon Friand Slice

MAKES ABOUT 18 PIECES

1¼ cups gluten-free icing sugar, plus extra to sprinkle (optional)

½ cup gluten-free self-raising flour

1 cup ground almonds

2 teaspoons finely grated lemon zest

4 egg whites, lightly whisked

150g butter or margarine, melted

150g frozen raspberries

{ GF }

Preheat the oven to 180°C. Grease and line a 16cm x 26cm slice pan with baking paper.

In a bowl, mix together the sifted icing sugar and flour. Stir in the ground almonds and lemon zest. Stir in the egg whites and butter or margarine and mix until just combined.

Pour into the prepared pan and sprinkle the raspberries over the top.

Bake for about 30 minutes, until a skewer inserted into the middle comes out clean.

Leave to cool in the pan for 10 minutes.

Dust over some extra icing sugar if desired. Cut into pieces to serve.

Store in an airtight container.

Fruit and Oat Slice

MAKES 18 PIECES

150g non-dairy spread

¾ cup brown sugar

3 tablespoons honey

¼ cup golden syrup

3½ cups rolled oats

⅔ cup ground hazelnuts

Filling

1 cup chopped dried fruit, such as apricots, cranberries or currants

¼ cup marmalade

finely grated zest of 1 lemon

{ DF EF V }

Preheat the oven to 180°C. Grease and line a 20cm x 30cm slice pan with baking paper.

Place the spread, sugar, honey and golden syrup in a microwave-proof bowl and microwave on High (100%) for 1½ minutes, or until the sugar has dissolved. Stir until well combined and smooth.

Stir in the rolled oats and hazelnuts and mix until well coated.

To make the filling, mix together the ingredients in a small bowl.

Press half the oat mixture into the bottom of the prepared pan. Gently drop the filling over the base and spread out as evenly as possible.

Press over the remaining oat mixture.

Bake for about 20 minutes, or until golden.

Allow to cool in the pan completely, before cutting into pieces.

Store in an airtight container.

Variation

Modify the filling by replacing the 1 cup of mixed fruit with chopped dates. Replace the marmalade with apricot jam.

Double Ginger Slice

MAKES 18 PIECES

Base

125g butter

¼ cup caster sugar

1 cup gluten-free plain flour

1 teaspoon gluten-free
baking powder

1 teaspoon ground ginger

½ teaspoon mixed spice

½ cup finely chopped
crystallised ginger, plus
extra to sprinkle (optional)

Topping

¼ cup butter

3 teaspoons ground ginger

3 tablespoons treacle

4 teaspoons water

3 cups gluten-free icing sugar

{ GF EF }

Preheat the oven to 180°C. Grease and line a 18cm x 30cm slice pan with baking paper, allowing extra paper to overhang.

Place the butter, sugar, sifted gluten-free flour, baking powder and spices in a food processor and process until the mix resembles breadcrumbs. Add the crystallised ginger and process again until crumbly.

Press the mixture evenly into the bottom of the prepared pan and bake for about 10 minutes, or until lightly browned. Remove from the oven.

While the base is cooking, prepare the topping. Place the butter, ginger, treacle and water in a microwave-proof bowl and microwave on High (100%) until the butter is melted. Do not allow it to boil as the mixture will curdle and separate.

Stir in the icing sugar and beat until smooth.

Spread the topping evenly over the hot base to cover completely.

Sprinkle with the extra chopped ginger if desired, and allow to cool completely in the pan.

Once cold, remove from the pan and cut into fingers to serve.

Store in an airtight container.

Wicked Chocolate, Almond and Pecan Slice

MAKES ABOUT 24 PIECES

Base

1 cup polenta

½ cup brown or coconut sugar

2 cups ground almonds

125g butter, softened

1 egg

Topping

1 cup chocolate chips

½ cup thread or desiccated coconut

1 cup pecan nuts, chopped

180g condensed milk

{ GF }

Preheat the oven to 180°C. Grease and line the base and sides of a 24cm square cake pan with baking paper.

To make the base, mix together the polenta, sugar and almonds. Rub in the butter until the mixture is a dry sandy consistency, then add the egg. Keep on mixing until it forms a dough. The dough can also be prepared in a food processor if you prefer.

Press into the base of the prepared pan.

Bake for about 15 minutes until golden brown.

Remove from the oven.

While the base is cooking, prepare the topping. In a bowl mix together the chocolate chips, coconut and pecan nuts.

Sprinkle this mixture evenly over the hot base, drizzle with the condensed milk and return to the oven for about 25 minutes. Watch it carefully as the coconut can burn easily. The top will be golden brown and set.

Cool completely in the pan before removing and cutting into small squares.

Store in an airtight container in the refrigerator.

Mini Brownie Bites

MAKES 36

160g non-dairy spread

150g dark chocolate, at least 72% cocoa, chopped

1½ cups sugar

1 teaspoon vanilla extract or essence

2 tablespoons ground flaxseed

¼ cup water

¼ teaspoon baking soda

½ cup cocoa

1½ cup plain flour

½ cup soy milk or other non-dairy milk substitute

{ DF EF V }

Preheat the oven to 180°C. Spray three 12-hole mini muffin trays with cooking spray.

Place the spread and chocolate in a microwave-proof bowl and microwave on High (100%) for about 1 minute. Stir until the chocolate and spread are well combined. Stir in the sugar and vanilla.

In a separate small microwave-proof bowl, combine the flaxseed and water together and microwave on High (100%) for 30 seconds. Stir this into the chocolate mixture.

Add the sifted baking soda, cocoa and flour to the chocolate mixture, then stir in the milk. Stir well to form a thick, smooth batter.

Divide the mixture between the muffin holes and bake for about 8 minutes.

Allow to cool in the tray for 5 minutes before transferring to a wire rack.

Store in an airtight container for up to three days.

Dark Chocolate Brownie

MAKES 16 PIECES

1½ tablespoons ground flaxseed

3 tablespoons water

¾ cup rice flour (brown or white)

1 cup ground almonds

2 tablespoons gluten-free cornflour

½ cup cocoa

¼ teaspoon baking soda

1 cup sugar

125g dark chocolate, at least 72% cocoa

80g non-dairy spread

1 teaspoon vanilla extract or essence

¼ cup almond milk or other non-dairy milk substitute

¼ cup finely chopped dairy-free white chocolate

½ cup finely chopped walnuts

{ GF DF EF V }

Preheat the oven to 180°C. Grease and line the base and sides of a 22cm square cake pan with baking paper.

In a small bowl, whisk together the flaxseed and water. Set aside.

In a separate bowl, combine the rice flour, almonds, cornflour, cocoa, baking soda and sugar.

In a separate microwave-proof bowl, place the chocolate and spread and microwave on High (100%) for 1 minute. Stir until the chocolate is melted and the mixture is smooth.

Add the flaxseed, vanilla and milk to the chocolate mixture and stir well. Pour this into the dry ingredients. Mix well – it will be stiff at first, but keep stirring until mixed.

Stir in the white chocolate and walnuts.

Spread the mixture into the prepared pan.

Bake for about 35 minutes. The brownie will still be quite soft in the middle.

Allow to cool completely in the pan.

Once cool, remove from the pan and cut into small pieces.

Store in an airtight container in the refrigerator.

Chocolate Chunk and Walnut Scones

MAKES 10–12

1 cup rice flour

1 cup tapioca flour

1 tablespoon gluten-free baking powder

1 teaspoon guar gum

½ teaspoon salt

75g butter, cubed

¾ cup roughly chopped dark chocolate, at least 60% cocoa, or chocolate chips

½ cup walnuts, finely chopped

about 1 cup milk

a little extra milk, to brush

{ GF EF }

Preheat the oven to 200°C. Line a baking tray with baking paper.

Sift the flours, baking powder, guar gum and salt into a bowl. Stir to combine.

Rub the butter into the dry ingredients until the mixture resembles breadcrumbs.

Stir in the chocolate and walnuts, then add enough milk to make a soft dough.

Sprinkle a little more tapioca flour onto the bench, tip out the dough and pat it into a long rectangle, about 30cm x 10cm. Cut into 10–12 pieces and place on the prepared tray. Allow enough room for them to spread. Brush milk on top of each scone.

Bake for about 12–15 minutes until golden brown.

Allow to cool on the tray for 5 minutes before serving with butter.

Cinnamon Date Scones

MAKES 10–12

1 cup rice flour

1 cup tapioca flour

1 tablespoon gluten-free
  baking powder

1 teaspoon guar gum

½ teaspoon salt

3 teaspoons caster sugar

½ teaspoon cinnamon

75g butter, cubed

1 cup chopped dates

about 1 cup milk

a little extra milk, to brush

a little extra caster sugar, to
  sprinkle (optional)

{ GF EF }

Preheat the oven to 200°C. Line a baking tray with baking paper.

Sift the flours, baking powder, guar gum, salt, sugar and cinnamon into a bowl. Stir to combine.

Rub the butter into the dry ingredients until the mixture resembles breadcrumbs.

Stir in the dates, then add enough milk to make a soft dough.

Sprinkle a little tapioca flour onto the bench, tip out the dough and pat it into a long rectangle, about 30cm x 10cm. Cut into 10–12 pieces and place on the prepared tray. Allow enough room for them to spread. Brush milk on top of each scone and sprinkle with sugar if desired.

Bake for about 12–15 minutes until golden brown.

Allow to cool on the tray for 5 minutes before serving with butter.

Apple and Raisin Scones

MAKES 10–12

1 cup rice flour

1 cup tapioca flour

1 tablespoon gluten-free baking powder

1 teaspoon guar gum

½ teaspoon salt

¼ cup brown sugar

½ teaspoon cinnamon

75g butter, cubed

1 apple, grated

½ cup raisins

about 1 cup milk

a little extra milk, to brush

a little extra brown sugar, to sprinkle (optional)

{ GF EF }

Preheat the oven to 200°C. Line a baking tray with baking paper.

Sift the flours, baking powder, guar gum, salt, sugar and cinnamon into a bowl. Stir to combine.

Rub the butter into the dry ingredients until the mixture resembles breadcrumbs.

Stir in the apple and raisins, then add enough milk to make a soft dough.

Sprinkle a little tapioca flour onto the bench, tip out the dough and pat it into a long rectangle, about 30cm x 10cm. Cut into 10–12 pieces and place on the prepared tray. Allow enough room for them to spread. Brush milk on top of each scone and sprinkle with sugar if desired.

Bake for about 12–15 minutes until golden brown.

Allow to cool on the tray for 5 minutes before serving with butter.

Cupcakes

Almond and Raspberry Chocolate Dessert Cakes

MAKES 6 LARGE CUPCAKES

120g butter

½ cup caster sugar

¼ cup cocoa

½ cup ground almonds

2 eggs, lightly whisked

2 tablespoons milk

Dark Chocolate Ganache
(see page 106)

1 punnet fresh raspberries,
to decorate

2 teaspoons gluten-free icing
sugar, to decorate (optional)

Preheat the oven to 180°C. Using cooking spray, grease one 6-hole jumbo muffin tray.

Place the butter, sugar and cocoa into a microwave-bowl and microwave on High (100%) for 1 minute. Stir and microwave again for 30 seconds. Stir until smooth and well combined.

Allow to cool for 5 minutes.

Stir in the ground almonds, eggs and milk. Stir until smooth.

Divide the mixture evenly between the muffin holes.

Bake for about 15 minutes until the cakes just feel firm when pressed lightly in the middle.

Allow to cool in the tray for 5 minutes before removing to a wire cake rack to cool completely.

Once cool, cut each cake in half horizontally. Use Dark Chocolate Ganache (see page 106) to sandwich the two halves together. Spread a little more ganache on top of each cake and arrange fresh raspberries over the top. Sprinkle with a little icing sugar if desired.

Vanilla Raspberry Cupcakes

MAKES 12

1 cup soy milk

1 teaspoon white vinegar

½ cup non-dairy spread

¾ cup caster sugar

2 teaspoons vanilla extract
   or essence

1¼ cups plain flour

2 tablespoons cornflour

¾ teaspoon baking powder

½ teaspoon baking soda

½ cup raspberries, thawed
   if frozen

Vanilla Frosting (see page 102)

{ DF
EF
V }

Preheat the oven to 180°C. Line one 12-hole muffin tray with cupcake papers.

In a small bowl, stir the soy milk and vinegar together. Set aside for 5 minutes to thicken.

In a larger bowl, add the non-dairy spread and the caster sugar and beat using electric beaters until pale in colour and very light.

Add the vanilla to the soy and vinegar mixture.

Sift the dry ingredients together. Add alternately to the creamed mixture with the thickened soy milk. Carefully scrape down the bowl with a spatula and mix for a final few seconds to make sure everything is well combined. Stir through the defrosted raspberries.

Divide the mixture evenly between the cupcake papers.

Bake for 20 minutes until the cakes just feel firm when pressed lightly in the middle.

Allow to cool in the tray for 5 minutes before removing to a wire cake rack to cool completely.

Once cool, ice with Vanilla Frosting and decorate as desired.

Ginger Cupcakes

MAKES 14–16

1⅓ cups gluten-free plain flour

½ cup brown sugar

½ cup caster sugar

2 teaspoons ground ginger

¼ teaspoon baking soda

1 tablespoon mixed spice

130g butter, melted and cooled

½ cup sour cream

1 tablespoon golden syrup

¼ cup crystallised ginger, finely chopped, plus extra to sprinkle

Ginger or Lemon Frosting (see page 102)

{ GF EF }

Preheat the oven to 180°C. Line two 12-hole muffin trays with cupcake papers.

Sift the flour, sugars, ginger, baking soda and mixed spice in a bowl. Stir to combine.

In a separate bowl, whisk together the butter, sour cream, golden syrup and ginger. Add this to the dry ingredients and mix well to form a smooth, glossy batter.

Divide the mixture evenly between the cupcake papers. They should be two-thirds full.

Bake for 20 minutes until the cakes just feel firm when pressed lightly in the middle.

Allow to cool in the trays for 5 minutes before removing to a wire cake rack to cool completely.

Once cool, ice with Ginger or Lemon Frosting and sprinkle with a little extra crystallised ginger. Alternatively, ice with Ginger Frosting and decorate with a gingerbread man, as shown in the photograph.

Carrot and Ginger Cupcakes

MAKES 36

500ml vegetable oil

3 cups brown sugar

6 eggs

600g carrots, peeled and grated

150g pecan nuts, chopped

125g sultanas

3⅓ cups gluten-free plain flour

1 teaspoon mixed spice

2 teaspoons baking soda

1 cup ground almonds

½ cup crystallised ginger, chopped

Cream Cheese Frosting (see page 103)

{ GF }

Preheat the oven to 180°C. Line three 12-hole muffin trays with cupcake papers.

In a large bowl, add the oil, brown sugar and eggs and beat with electric beaters until the mixture is creamy and pale.

Using a big wooden spoon, stir in the carrots, nuts and sultanas until the ingredients are well coated in the egg mixture.

Sift the flour, spice and baking soda together. Stir into the carrot mixture and add the ground almonds and ginger. Keep using the wooden spoon and stir until well combined.

Scoop the mixture into the cupcake papers using a half-cup measure.

Bake for 25 minutes.

Allow to cool in the trays for 5 minutes. Remove the cakes to a wire rack to finish cooling.

Once cool, ice with Cream Cheese Frosting and decorate with a little flower (see page 112).

Banana and Cinnamon Mini Cupcakes

MAKES 24 MINI CUPCAKES

2 tablespoons sour cream

1 banana, mashed

½ cup brown sugar

1 egg

1 cup gluten-free self-raising flour

2 tablespoons butter, softened

1 teaspoon cinnamon

Cream Cheese Frosting (see page 103) or Lemon Frosting (see page 102)

 GF

Preheat the oven to 180°C. Line two 12-hole mini muffin trays with small cupcake papers.

Place all the ingredients in a bowl. Using electric beaters, beat on low speed until combined, then beat on high speed for 2 minutes.

Divide the mixture evenly between the cupcake papers.

Bake for 12 minutes.

Allow to cool in the trays for 5 minutes before removing to a wire cake rack to cool completely.

Once cool, ice with Cream Cheese Frosting or Lemon Frosting and decorate with a small yellow and an orange butterfly (see page 114).

Chocolate Cupcakes

MAKES 24

175g butter

1½ cups caster sugar

3 eggs

1 teaspoon vanilla extract
   or essence

¾ cup cocoa

2 cups gluten-free plain flour

2 teaspoons gluten-free
   baking powder

1 cup milk

Chocolate Frosting
   (see page 103)

{ GF }

Preheat the oven to 190°C. Line two 12-hole muffin trays with cupcake papers.

Place the butter, sugar, eggs and vanilla in a bowl. Using electric beaters, beat on high speed until the mixture is very light and fluffy.

Sift in the cocoa, flour and baking powder, then add the milk and beat on low speed until the mixture is combined. Increase the speed to high and beat for 30 seconds.

Divide the mixture evenly between the cupcake papers.

Bake for about 18 minutes until the cakes just feel firm when pressed lightly in the middle.

Allow to cool in the trays for 5 minutes before removing to a wire cake rack to cool completely.

Once cool, ice with Chocolate Frosting and decorate with chocolate curls.

Variation

These cakes can be baked in mini cake cylinders as mini cakes. They take about 25 minutes to bake.

Orange Cupcakes

MAKES 24

2 cups caster sugar

250g butter, softened

finely grated zest and juice of
2 large oranges

6 eggs

2 cups tapioca flour

1½ cups rice flour

1 tablespoon gluten-free
baking powder

2 teaspoons guar gum

water

2 tablespoons lemon juice

Orange Frosting
(see page 102)

{ GF }

Preheat the oven to 180°C. Line two 12-hole muffin trays with cupcake papers.

Place the sugar, butter, orange zest and eggs in a large bowl and beat with electric beaters until light, fluffy and pale in colour.

Add the sifted flours, baking powder and guar gum.

Make the orange juice up to 1 cup with water. Add to the bowl, along with the lemon juice and beat until just mixed, otherwise the batter will become tough and the cakes will shrink.

Divide the mixture evenly between the cupcake papers. They should be two-thirds full.

Bake for about 10–12 minutes, until the cakes just feel firm when pressed lightly in the middle. If a toothpick inserted into the cakes comes out clean, the cakes are ready.

Allow to cool in the trays for 5 minutes before removing to a wire cake rack to cool completely.

Ice with Orange Frosting and decorate with an orange flower (see page 116).

Sticky Date Cupcakes

MAKES 24

400g dates, chopped

700ml water

2 teaspoons vanilla extract
or essence

1 tablespoon baking soda

180g dairy-free spread

1 cup brown sugar

4 eggs, lightly whisked

3⅓ cups gluten-free plain flour

Dairy-free Caramel Frosting
(see page 104)

{ GF DF }

Preheat the oven to 180°C. Line two 12-hole muffin trays with cupcake papers.

Place the dates and water into a medium-sized saucepan and cook for 5 minutes, or until soft. Stir in the vanilla and baking soda. Set aside to cool.

Beat together the spread and sugar until pale and creamy. Gradually add the eggs. Stir in the cooled date mixture. Fold in the flour.

Divide the mixture evenly between the cupcake papers.

Bake for 20–25 minutes until the cakes just feel firm when pressed lightly in the middle.

Allow to cool in the trays for 5 minutes before removing to a wire cake rack to cool completely.

Once cool, ice with Dairy-free Caramel Frosting and decorate as desired.

Zucchini and Apple Cupcakes

MAKES 18

2 cups sugar

2 eggs

120ml vegetable oil

2 cups plain flour

1 teaspoon cinnamon

½ teaspoon ground nutmeg

½ teaspoon salt

1½ teaspoons baking soda

250g zucchini, grated

250g cooking apples, peeled, cored and grated

115g chopped walnuts

Vanilla Frosting (see page 102)

 { DF }

Preheat the oven to 175°C. Line two 12-hole muffin trays with 18 cupcake papers.

In a large bowl, mix together the sugar and eggs. Add the oil and mix well.

Sift in the flour, cinnamon, nutmeg, salt and baking soda. Stir in the zucchini, apples and nuts.

Divide the mixture evenly between the cupcake papers.

Bake for 25 minutes until the cakes just feel firm when pressed lightly in the middle.

Allow to cool in the trays for 10 minutes before removing to a wire cake rack to cool completely.

Once cool, ice with Vanilla Frosting and add a little cinnamon if desired.

Almond and Vanilla Cupcakes

MAKES 18

180g butter

1 cup sugar

4 eggs

½ cup milk

1 teaspoon vanilla extract
  or essence

1½ cups ground almonds

½ cup coconut flour

3 teaspoons gluten-free baking
  powder

gluten-free icing sugar,
  to sprinkle

whipped cream, to serve

fresh fruit, to serve

 { GF }

Preheat the oven to 180°C. Line two 12-hole muffin trays with 18 cupcake papers.

Cream the butter and sugar until smooth. Add eggs, one at a time, and beat well after each addition. Add milk and vanilla and mix until combined.

In a separate bowl, sift in the ground almonds, flour and baking powder.

Stir the dry ingredients into the liquid ingredients and beat until creamy.

Divide the mixture evenly between the cupcake papers.

Bake for about 15 minutes, until the cakes just feel firm when pressed lightly in the middle.

Allow to cool in the trays for 5 minutes before removing to a wire cake rack to cool completely.

Sprinkle with a little icing sugar and serve with a swirl of whipped cream and fresh fruit.

Rich Dark Chocolate Cupcakes

MAKES 24

100g dark chocolate, at least 72% cocoa

1 cup rice flour

½ cup gluten-free cornflour

⅓ cup potato flour

¾ cup cocoa

2 teaspoons gluten-free baking powder

1 teaspoon baking soda

2 eggs

1½ cups caster sugar

50g butter, melted

200g vanilla yoghurt

160ml milk

1 teaspoon vanilla extract or essence

Chocolate Frosting (see page 103)

{ GF }

Preheat the oven to 170°C. Line two 12-hole muffin trays with cupcake papers.

Place the chocolate in a microwave-proof bowl and microwave on High (100%) until melted, about 1–2 minutes, stirring halfway through the cooking time. Alternatively, melt in a bowl over simmering water. Allow to cool slightly.

In a large bowl, sift the flours, cocoa, baking powder and baking soda.

In a separate jug, whisk together the eggs and sugar. Add the butter, yoghurt, milk and vanilla. Mix well.

Pour the egg mixture into the flour mixture. Using electric beaters, beat on low speed for 2 minutes or until the mixture is pale in colour. Mix in the melted chocolate.

Divide the mixture evenly between the cupcake papers. They should only be about half full as these cupcakes rise a lot.

Bake for 18 minutes until the cakes just feel firm when pressed lightly in the middle.

Allow to cool in the trays for 5 minutes before removing to a wire cake rack to cool completely.

Once cool, ice with Chocolate Frosting and decorate with Chocolate Cut-outs (see page 122).

Chocolate Rice Milk Cupcakes

MAKES 12

1 cup rice milk

1 teaspoon white vinegar

¾ cup caster sugar

80ml vegetable oil

1 teaspoon vanilla extract or essence

1 cup plain flour

½ cup cocoa

½ teaspoon baking powder

½ teaspoon baking soda

Chocolate Frosting (see page 103)

{ DF EF V }

Preheat the oven to 180°C. Line one 12-hole muffin tray with cupcake papers.

Whisk together the rice milk and vinegar in a bowl and leave for a couple of minutes to thicken. The mixture will resemble runny yoghurt.

Mix the sugar, oil and vanilla into the thickened milk.

Sift the flour, cocoa, baking powder and baking soda over the milk mixture and combine the ingredients gradually with a whisk. Beat well to make sure there are no lumps.

Divide the mixture evenly between the cupcake papers. They should be two-thirds full.

Bake for 20 minutes until the cakes just feel firm when pressed lightly in the middle.

Allow to cool in the tray for 10 minutes before removing to a wire cake rack to cool completely.

Once cool, ice with Chocolate Frosting and decorate as desired.

Hummingbird Cupcakes

MAKES 30

1 x 900g can crushed pineapple in natural juice

4 bananas, mashed

2¼ cups brown sugar

375ml vegetable oil

4 eggs

1 teaspoon baking soda

2 teaspoons baking powder

1 teaspoon mixed spice

3 cups plain flour

1 cup long thread coconut

Dairy-free Vanilla or Dairy-free Lemon Frosting (see page 104)

{ DF }

Preheat the oven to 200°C. Line three 12-hole muffin trays with 30 cupcake papers.

Place the pineapple in a sieve over a bowl and press down to remove the juice. Reserve half a cup of juice to add into the cake mixture.

Place all the ingredients, including the drained, crushed pineapple and the reserved juice, into a large bowl. Beat well, using either a wooden spoon or electric beaters until well combined.

Divide the mixture evenly between the cupcake papers.

Bake for about 22 minutes until the cakes just feel firm when pressed lightly in the middle.

Allow to cool in the trays for 5 minutes before removing to a wire cake rack to finish cooling.

Once cool, ice with Dairy-free Vanilla or Dairy-free Lemon Frosting. Make three brightly coloured flowers (see page 116) and arrange on the cakes.

Hazelnut and Coffee Cupcakes

MAKES 12

⅔ cup rice or almond milk

1 tablespoon ground flaxseed

1 cup plain flour

1 teaspoon baking powder

½ teaspoon baking soda

1 teaspoon cinnamon

⅓ cup ground hazelnuts

½ cup firmly packed brown sugar

½ cup vegetable oil

1 tablespoon espresso or 2 teaspoons instant coffee granules dissolved in 1 tablespoon boiling water

1 teaspoon vanilla extract or essence

Dairy-free Coffee Frosting (see page 104)

{ DF EF V }

Preheat the oven to 180°C. Line one 12-hole muffin tray with cupcake papers.

Place the rice or almond milk and flaxseed in a small bowl and stir to combine.

In a separate bowl, mix together the sifted flour, baking powder, baking soda and cinnamon. Stir in the nuts and sugar.

Add the oil, coffee and vanilla to the milk mixture. Pour this into the dry ingredients and stir to combine.

Stir well until the mixture is smooth.

Divide the mixture evenly between the cupcake papers.

Bake for about 18 minutes until the cakes just feel firm when pressed lightly in the middle.

Allow to cool in the tray for 5 minutes before removing to a wire cake rack to cool completely.

Once cool, ice with Dairy-free Coffee Frosting and decorate with Caramelised Nuts (see page 124).

Strawberry Cupcakes

MAKES 36

220g non-dairy spread

2 teaspoons vanilla extract or essence

1½ cups caster sugar

2 cups self-raising flour

2 eggs

375ml water

200g fresh or frozen strawberries, chopped

Dairy-free Vanilla Frosting (see page 104)

{ DF }

Preheat the oven to 180°C. Line three 12-hole muffin trays with cupcake papers.

Place the spread, vanilla, sugar, flour, eggs and water in a bowl. Using electric beaters, beat on low speed for 1 minute until blended.

Increase the speed to high. Beat for a further 4 minutes or until the mixture has thickened. Stir in the strawberries.

Divide the mixture evenly between the cupcake papers.

Bake for 12–15 minutes until golden brown.

Allow to cool in the trays for 5 minutes before removing to a wire cake rack to cool completely.

Once cool, ice with Dairy-free Vanilla Frosting and decorate as desired.

Lime and Coconut Cupcakes

MAKES 12

⅓ cup vegetable oil

1 cup coconut cream

1 cup sugar

½ cup soy milk

1 teaspoon lime juice

1 tablespoon finely grated lime zest

1 cup plain flour

¾ cup coconut flour

½ teaspoon baking powder

½ teaspoon baking soda

Lime drizzle

1 cup icing sugar

about 2 teaspoons lime juice

{ DF EF V }

Preheat the oven to 180°C. Line one 12-hole muffin tray with cupcake papers.

Place the oil, coconut cream, sugar, soy milk and lime juice and zest in a large bowl and mix well.

Sift in the flours, baking powder and baking soda and stir to combine. Mix until smooth.

Divide the mixture evenly between the cupcake papers.

Bake for about 20 minutes until the cakes just feel firm when pressed lightly in the middle.

Allow to cool in the tray for 5 minutes before removing to a wire cake rack to cool completely.

To make the lime drizzle, stir the icing sugar and lime juice together until smooth and just dropping consistency. Drizzle over the cooled cupcakes. Alternatively, ice with Dairy-free Lemon Frosting (see page 104) and decorate as desired.

Hazelnut and Chocolate Friands

MAKES 12

1½ cups gluten-free icing sugar, plus a little extra to serve

½ cup rice flour

¼ cup cocoa

1 cup ground hazelnuts (or use pecans or almonds)

5 egg whites, lightly beaten

185g butter, melted and cooled

{ GF }

Preheat the oven to 180°C. Using cooking spray, grease one 12-hole friand or muffin tray.

Sift the icing sugar, rice flour and cocoa into a bowl, then stir in the hazelnuts. Mix to combine.

Add the beaten egg whites and cooled butter and stir well to combine.

Divide the mixture evenly between the holes.

Bake for about 15 minutes until the cakes just feel firm when pressed lightly in the middle.

Allow to cool in the tray for 5 minutes before removing to a wire cake rack to cool completely.

Sift over a little extra icing sugar before serving.

Cakes

Birthday Black Forest Cake

100g dark chocolate, at least 72% cocoa

125g non-dairy spread

1 cup hot water

1¼ cups brown sugar

1 cup gluten-free plain flour

½ cup rice flour

3 teaspoons gluten-free baking powder

¼ cup cocoa

½ cup ground almonds

3 eggs

Filling

¼ cup Kirsch

600ml thickened cream, whipped

1 x 880g jar pitted dark sour cherries

Topping

100g dark chocolate, at least 72% cocoa

3 tablespoons cream

{ GF }

Preheat the oven to 180°C. Grease and line the base of a round 20cm springform cake pan with baking paper.

Place the chocolate, spread and hot water in a microwave-proof bowl and microwave on High (100%) for 1 minute. Stir and microwave again for another 1 minute or until chocolate and spread melt. Stir until smooth and well combined.

Stir in the sugar. Pour the chocolate mixture into a larger bowl and using a whisk, stir in the sifted flours, baking powder, cocoa and ground almonds. Whisk to combine and leave to cool for 5 minutes.

Using electric beaters, beat the eggs in another bowl for 5 minutes until thick and pale. The mixture will form a ribbon trail when the beaters are lifted from the bowl. Fold the eggs lightly but thoroughly through the chocolate mixture.

Pour the mixture into the prepared pan. Bake for 1 hour or until the cake is cooked when tested with a skewer.

Allow cake to cool in the pan.

Once cold, cut the cake into three even layers, using a serrated knife.

Sprinkle 2 tablespoons of the Kirsch over the bottom layer, then spread with half the cream. Dot with well-drained cherries. Repeat with the second layer of cake and finish with the top layer.

Melt the dark chocolate and cream together until smooth and glossy, then spread over the top of the cake. Dot with a few chocolate curls or extra cherries if desired.

Cranberry and Nut Dessert Cake

1½ cups dried cranberries

3 cups water

1 teaspoon cinnamon

¾ cup ground hazelnuts

1¾ cups ground almonds

1 cup sugar

1 teaspoon gluten-free baking powder

5 eggs

1 teaspoon vanilla extract or essence

a little gluten-free icing sugar, to serve

{ GF DF }

Preheat the oven to 170°C. Grease and line the base of a round 22cm springform cake pan with baking paper.

Place the cranberries, water and cinnamon in a saucepan and bring to the boil. Lower the heat to a simmer and cook uncovered for 1 hour. Remove from the heat and set aside to cool.

Drain the liquid from the fruit.

Place the ground nuts, sugar and baking powder in a bowl and mix to combine.

Place the cranberries into a food processor and pulse for 30 seconds. Add in the eggs one at a time, pulsing for 10 seconds after each egg. Add in the vanilla. The mixture will be frothy.

Add the nut mixture and process until well combined. Scrape down the bowl once during this time.

Pour the mixture into the prepared pan. Bake for about 1 hour or until the cake is cooked when tested with a skewer.

Allow cake to cool in the pan for 10 minutes before removing to a wire cake rack to cool completely.

Dust over a little extra icing sugar to serve and decorate with hazelnuts if desired. This cake is also delicious served with mascarpone or Greek yoghurt.

Rich Chocolate and Pecan Cake

1 cup unsweetened applesauce, purchase from supermarket or stew 4 green apples

½ cup coconut sugar

1 teaspoon vanilla extract or essence

¾ cup plain flour

⅓ cup cocoa

2 teaspoons baking powder

½ teaspoon baking soda

½ cup vegan chocolate chips (see chocolate, page 8)

⅓ cup chopped pecan nuts

Icing sugar or Dairy-free Chocolate Frosting (see page 105)

{ DF EF V }

Preheat the oven to 180°C. Grease and line the base and sides of a 20cm square cake pan with baking paper.

Place the applesauce, sugar and vanilla into a bowl and stir to combine. Add the sifted flour, cocoa, baking powder and baking soda, then stir in the chocolate chips and nuts.

Stir gently until just combined.

Pour the mixture into the prepared pan. Bake for about 25–30 minutes until the middle is firm.

Allow cake to cool in the pan before serving.

Once cool, dust with icing sugar, or for a more decadent option ice with Dairy-free Chocolate Frosting.

Chocolate and Orange Cake

2 whole oranges

200g dark chocolate, at least 60% cocoa

100g butter

8 eggs

1½ cups caster sugar

2 cups ground almonds

Dark Chocolate Ganache (see page 106)

 { GF }

Preheat the oven to 180°C. Grease and line a 20cm round cake pan with baking paper.

Place the oranges in a saucepan and cover with water. Place a lid on the saucepan. Bring to the boil, then reduce the heat and simmer for 30 minutes until the oranges are very soft. Remove from the heat and set aside to cool.

Once cool, place the oranges in a food processor and purée until a rough paste is formed.

Place the chocolate and butter in a microwave-proof bowl and microwave on High (100%) for 1 minute. Stir and microwave again for another 30 seconds to 1 minute or until the chocolate and butter melt. Stir until smooth. Set aside to cool.

Place the eggs and sugar in a bowl and beat together until well mixed and pale in colour.

Gently mix in the almonds, orange purée and chocolate and butter mixture. Stir until just combined.

Pour the mixture into the prepared pan. Bake for about 1½ hours or until the cake is cooked when tested with a skewer.

Allow cake to cool in the pan for 20 minutes before removing to a wire cake rack to cool completely.

Once cool, ice with Dark Chocolate Ganache.

Chocolate Cake

1¼ cups plain flour

¾ cup cocoa

3 teaspoons baking soda

2 cups caster sugar

1 cup brown sugar

2 teaspoons instant coffee granules

1 cup vegetable oil

¾ cup water

1 tablespoon vanilla extract or essence

Dairy-free Chocolate Frosting (see page 105)

{ DF EF V }

Preheat the oven to 180°C. Grease and line a 22cm round cake pan with baking paper.

Place the flour, cocoa, baking soda, sugars and coffee into a large bowl and mix together using a whisk to break up any cocoa lumps.

Add the oil, water and vanilla. Mix together well until a smooth batter is formed.

Pour the mixture into the prepared pan. Bake for about 1 hour or until the cake is cooked when tested with a skewer. If the top begins to brown too much before the cake is fully cooked, cover with a piece of aluminium foil.

Allow cake to cool in the pan for 10 minutes before removing to a wire cake rack to cool completely.

Once cool, ice with Dairy-free Chocolate Frosting and top with chocolate-dipped strawberries.

Vanilla Cake

¼ cup water

2 tablespoons vegetable oil

2 teaspoons baking powder

3¾ cups plain flour

1¾ cups caster sugar

1 teaspoon vanilla extract
or essence

2 tablespoons non-dairy
spread

315ml water, extra

2½ teaspoons baking powder,
extra

Dairy-free Vanilla Frosting
(see page 104)

{ DF EF V }

Preheat the oven to 180°C. Grease and line a 20cm round cake pan with baking paper.

Place the water, oil and first measure of baking powder into a bowl. Using electric beaters, beat until combined, about 30 seconds.

Add all the remaining ingredients and beat on low speed until just combined.

Increase the speed to high and beat until the mixture is smooth and lighter in colour, about 3 minutes.

Pour the mixture into the prepared pan. Bake for about 40 minutes or until the cake is cooked when tested with a skewer. If the top begins to brown too much before the cake is fully cooked, cover with a piece of aluminium foil.

Allow cake to cool in the pan for 10 minutes before removing to a wire cake rack to cool completely.

Once cool, ice with Dairy-free Vanilla Frosting.

To decorate, make a selection of butterflies (see page 114) and allow them to dry. Make a bow (see page 120) and use to decorate the middle of the cake. Arrange the butterflies randomly over the cake.

Fruitcake

125g sultanas

100g currants

100g dried cranberries

500ml water

500g pumpkin, peeled, cooked, mashed and cooled

finely grated zest of 2 lemons

65ml vegetable oil

375g gluten-free plain flour

3 teaspoons gluten-free baking powder

1 teaspoon cinnamon

1 teaspoon mixed spice

½ teaspoon ground ginger

{ GF DF EF V }

Preheat the oven to 170°C. Grease and line a 20cm round cake pan with baking paper.

Place the dried fruit and the water into a saucepan and bring to the boil. Lower the heat and simmer for 5 minutes. Remove from the heat and stir in the pumpkin, lemon zest and oil. Set aside to cool.

Once cool, sift in the flour, baking powder, cinnamon, mixed spice and ground ginger.

Spread the mixture into the prepared pan and smooth the top with a spoon. Bake for about 1½ hours or until the cake is cooked when tested with a skewer.

Allow cake to cool in the pan for 10 minutes before removing to a wire cake rack to cool completely.

Ice with purchased rolled fondant and decorate as desired.

Frostings and Toppings

– 102 –
Vanilla Frosting

Cinnamon Frosting	Lemon Frosting
Coffee Frosting	Orange Frosting
Coloured Frosting	Pistachio Frosting
Ginger Frosting	

– 103 –
Chocolate Frosting
Cream Cheese Frosting
Vegan Cream Cheese Frosting

– 104 –
Dairy-free Vanilla Frosting

Dairy-free Caramel Frosting	Dairy-free Lemon Frosting
Dairy-free Coffee Frosting	Dairy-free Orange Frosting
Dairy-free Ginger Frosting	

– 105 –
Dairy-free Vanilla Yoghurt Frosting
Dairy-free Chocolate Frosting

– 106 –
Dark Chocolate Ganache
Royal Icing

Vanilla Frosting

250g butter
800g gluten-free icing sugar, sifted
¼ cup milk
1 teaspoon vanilla extract or essence

Place all the ingredients into a bowl. Using electric beaters, beat on low speed until combined, then increase the speed to medium and continue to beat until the frosting lightens in colour and becomes fluffy.

You might need to add a little more milk, 1 tablespoon at a time, if the mixture is too stiff.

Store in an airtight container. This frosting will keep for 3 days out of the fridge or 1 week in the fridge.

You might need to gently soften the refrigerated frosting for 15 seconds in the microwave before piping onto cupcakes.

Variations

Cinnamon Frosting: Add 1½ teaspoons cinnamon to the mixture.

Coffee Frosting: Omit the vanilla and add 10g instant coffee granules, dissolved in a little hot water. Add milk to this to make up to ¼ cup liquid in total, then add to the mixture.

Coloured Frosting: Add a small amount liquid food colouring or paste into the mixture until the desired colour is reached.

Ginger Frosting: Add 2 teaspoons ground ginger to the mixture.

Lemon Frosting: Omit the vanilla and add the finely grated zest of 1 lemon. Squeeze the juice from the lemon and measure this with the milk to make ¼ cup liquid in total.

Orange Frosting: Omit the vanilla and add 2 teaspoons finely grated orange zest.

Pistachio Frosting: Add in ½ cup finely ground pistachio nuts.

Chocolate Frosting

270g butter

800g gluten-free icing sugar

50g cocoa, sifted

1 teaspoon vanilla extract
or essence

¼ cup milk

Place the butter and sifted icing sugar in a bowl and beat using electric beaters until combined. Add the cocoa, vanilla and milk. Continue to beat until very fluffy and lighter in colour.

Store in an airtight container. This frosting will keep for 2 days out of the fridge or 1 week in the fridge.

Cream Cheese Frosting

100g butter, softened

450g cream cheese

2 teaspoons lemon juice

800g gluten-free icing sugar,
sifted

Soften the cream cheese in the microwave on Low (50%) for 30 seconds. Place the butter, cream cheese and lemon juice in a bowl and using electric beaters, cream the mixture.

Add the icing sugar into the cheese and butter gradually, about a quarter of a cup at a time. The frosting will become light and creamy, and develop the consistency of peanut butter.

Store in an airtight container in the fridge and remove an hour ahead of when it is required, to soften the frosting.

Vegan Cream Cheese Frosting

60g non-dairy spread

60g vegan cream cheese

2 cups gluten-free icing sugar,
sifted

1 teaspoon vanilla extract
or essence

1 teaspoon finely grated
lemon zest

Using electric beaters, cream the spread and cheese together until just combined.

Gradually beat in the sifted icing sugar. Beat until light and creamy. Stir in the vanilla and lemon zest.

Store in an airtight container. This frosting will keep for 1 week in the fridge.

Dairy-free Vanilla Frosting

250g non-dairy spread
800g gluten-free icing sugar
2 tablespoons hot water
1 teaspoon vanilla extract or essence

Using electric beaters, beat the spread in a bowl until light and fluffy.

Gradually beat in the sifted icing sugar, beating on low speed until combined.

Beat in the water and vanilla until just combined.

Store in an airtight container. This frosting will keep for 2 days out of the fridge or 1 week in the fridge.

Variations

Dairy-free Caramel Frosting: Add 2 tablespoons of caramel made by melting together ¼ cup sugar and 2 tablespoons non-dairy spread. Cook until golden brown. Cool completely before adding to frosting.

Dairy-free Coffee Frosting: Omit the vanilla and add 10g instant coffee granules, dissolved in a little hot water.

Dairy-free Ginger Frosting: Omit the vanilla and add 3 teaspoons ground ginger.

Dairy-free Lemon Frosting: Omit the vanilla and add the finely grated zest of 2 lemons.

Dairy-free Orange Frosting: Omit the vanilla and add 2 teaspoons finely grated orange zest.

Dairy-free Vanilla Yoghurt Frosting

200g non-dairy spread

600g gluten-free icing sugar

2 tablespoons soy or rice milk

2 teaspoons vanilla extract
  or essence

50ml vanilla soy yoghurt

Using electric beaters, cream the spread in a large bowl for about 2 minutes until fluffy.

Gradually beat in the sifted icing sugar, beating on low speed until combined.

Turn the speed to high and beat in the milk, vanilla and yoghurt. Continue to beat until the mixture is smooth and creamy.

Chill slightly before use.

Dairy-free Chocolate Frosting

125g non-dairy spread

500g gluten-free icing sugar

80g cocoa

1 tablespoon soy milk

2 teaspoons vanilla extract
  or essence

Using electric beaters, cream the spread in a bowl until fluffy.

Add half the sifted icing sugar and half the cocoa, and 2 teaspoons of the milk. Beat until the icing begins to turn lighter in colour and increase in volume. Add the remaining icing sugar, cocoa and milk, and the vanilla. Beat again until all the ingredients are well combined and the mixture is very creamy. If the frosting is too stiff add a little more milk.

Dark Chocolate Ganache

400g dark chocolate, at least
60% cocoa

375ml cream

Place the cream and chocolate in a microwave-proof bowl. Microwave on High (100%) for about 4 minutes until the cream is almost boiling.

Remove from the microwave and use a whisk to gently combine the chocolate and cream.

Keep stirring until it is well mixed and glossy.

Leave in a covered bowl, unrefrigerated, overnight to thicken.

Store in an airtight container. This ganache will keep for 3 days out of the fridge or 1 week in the fridge.

Royal Icing

1 egg white

about 2 cups gluten-free
icing sugar

Beat the egg white in a small bowl using electric beaters until foamy.

Gradually beat in the icing sugar, starting with 1 cup, then add the remainder a spoonful at a time. You may need more or less depending on the size of the egg. The icing is ready when it forms soft dropping peaks off the beater.

Store in an airtight container.

Decorations

Modelling Paste

2½ cups gluten-free icing sugar

½ cup gluten-free cornflour

3 teaspoons gum tragacanth

5 teaspoons cold water

2 teaspoons gelatine

2 teaspoons glucose syrup

3 teaspoons white vegetable shortening

1 large egg white

food colouring paste

{ Note: this is not suitable for use on vegan cakes as it contains gelatine }

Sift icing sugar and cornflour into the bowl of a stand mixer. Sprinkle gum tragacanth on top. Set the bowl in a pan of boiling water and cover with a cloth.

Put the water and gelatine in the top of a double boiler and allow the gelatine to soften for 5 minutes.

Bring the water in the bottom of the double boiler to a simmer. Set the gelatine mixture on top and add the glucose and shortening to the gelatine mixture. Stir until the shortening is completely melted.

Pour the gelatine mixture into the icing sugar and cornflour mixture and beat on low speed until all the ingredients are combined. Beat on high speed for 5–10 minutes, or until the dough looks stringy.

Wrap the paste in plastic food wrap or place in an airtight plastic bag and refrigerate for 24 hours. Before using, knead the paste — the warmth of your hands will soften it. Add a dab of shortening and work it in to the paste to make it pliable, if required.

Roll the modelling paste out on a surface dusted with cornflour. Dust the rolling pin with cornflour to prevent sticking.

Use food colouring paste to tint modelling paste. Add a tiny amount at a time, using a toothpick. Knead the colour into the paste until the colour is uniform throughout. Some colours tend to darken over time, so tint the modelling paste slightly lighter than the desired colour. After you add colour, you may find that the modelling paste becomes too soft. If that happens, allow it to sit for 15 minutes until it returns to its normal texture. Modelling paste dries quickly when exposed to air, so only remove what you need from the plastic.

Roll out thinly to make leaves, butterflies and petals for flowers.

Store the modelling paste wrapped in a plastic bag inside an airtight container. The paste will keep for 4 weeks at least if well wrapped.

Using Silicon Moulds

food colouring paste

modelling paste (see page 110)

cornflour

silicon moulds of your choice

Mix a little food colouring paste into the modelling paste. Mix well to evenly blend the colour.

Rub a little cornflour into the silicon mould. When using dark-coloured modelling paste be careful not to use too much cornflour, as this will leave white powder on your finished pieces. If this does happen you can wipe off the excess, once the decoration has dried, with a piece of damp absorbent kitchen paper.

Press the modelling paste into the mould, gently pushing it into the small spaces of the mould. Peel away the mould gently to expose the shape.

Leave the decorations to dry overnight.

Note: for vegan-friendly decorations, use ready-made fondant that contains no gelatine. These decorations take 2–3 days to dry completely before they can be used on cakes or cupcakes.

Variations

Multicoloured flowers can be made by using a small ball of modelling paste and placing it into the middle of the flower shape in the mould. Gently place the second piece of modelling paste over the middle and gently push to join the pieces. Peel away the mould.

Gingerbread people can be made by using a small ball of modelling paste and placing it into the middle of a silicon gingerbread man mould. Peel away the mould and ice as desired.

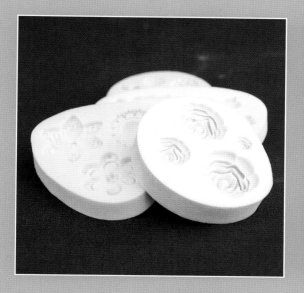
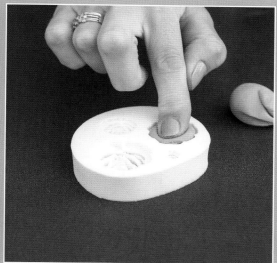
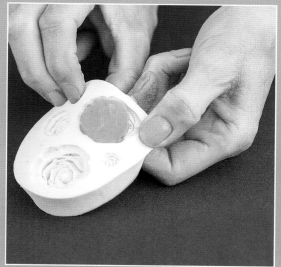
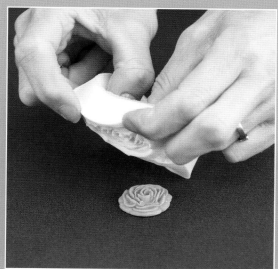

Butterflies

food colouring paste

modelling paste (see page 110)

cornflour

toothpicks

butterfly mould

rolling pin and silicon board

cardboard, folded into a
concertina

Use a toothpick to add a little food colouring paste to the modelling paste. Mix well to evenly blend the colour. Dust your work surface or silicon board with a little cornflour and roll out the paste thinly. Lightly dust the butterfly mould with cornflour and press it down into the modelling paste. As you remove each butterfly from the mould, gently bend it in half and place it in the cardboard support. Repeat to make as many butterflies as required. Allow to dry overnight.

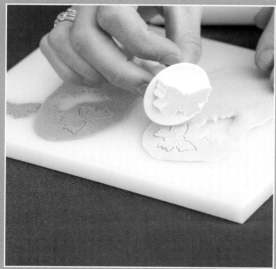

Flowers

food colouring paste

modelling paste (see page 110)

cornflour

toothpicks

flower cutters, such as gerbera, daisy or other 5-petal cutter (6–8cm)

rolling pin and silicon board

small muffin tray or artist palate to dry flowers

small amount of royal icing (see page 106)

Use a toothpick to add a little food colouring paste to the modelling paste. Mix well to evenly blend the colour.

Dust your work surface or silicon board with a little cornflour and roll out the paste thinly.

Use a cutter to cut out flower shapes. Soften the edges of the 5-petal flowers between your thumb and forefinger to ruffle slightly. Place in the muffin tray to dry.

Leave the flowers to dry overnight, and make sure they are well dried as the petals are fragile and break off easily.

Once dry, pipe a little royal icing into the middle of each flower. Allow to dry again overnight before using on your cakes.

These decorations store very well in a cardboard box between tissue paper and last indefinitely.

How to Make a Paper Piping Bag

Steps 1 & 2

Cut a 30cm square piece of baking paper. Cut this in half to form two triangles. Hold one of the triangles in your left hand at the middle of the longest side. Your right hand is holding the point opposite this, the apex of the triangle. Move your right hand over to the right corner and curl it over to the top corner to form a cone.

Steps 3 & 4

Move your left hand to the left corner and roll it around until all corners meet at the top back of the cone. Adjust the shape of the piping bag by sliding the points backwards and forwards between your thumb and fingers until a sharp point is formed at the bottom of the cone.

Steps 5

Fold the corners to the inside of the cone, and secure by stapling or tearing each side by the seam and folding the flap inside.

Steps 6

Fill the bag by holding it in one hand and using a knife or small spoon. Fold over the opening away from the seam to form a neat seal.

Don't overfill the piping bag or the icing will squeeze out through the top as you pipe. It should be about half full.

Snip off the point of the piping bag to the thickness you require for piping. It is better to start with a small opening and make it bigger, if necessary.

Holding the bag in your favoured hand, place the point of the bag between your thumb and fingers. Use the thumb to control the flow of the icing. Use the other hand to direct the bag.

It will take practice to master both making and using a piping bag, but the rewards will make the effort worthwhile. Alternatively, you can buy reusable piping bags from specialty suppliers.

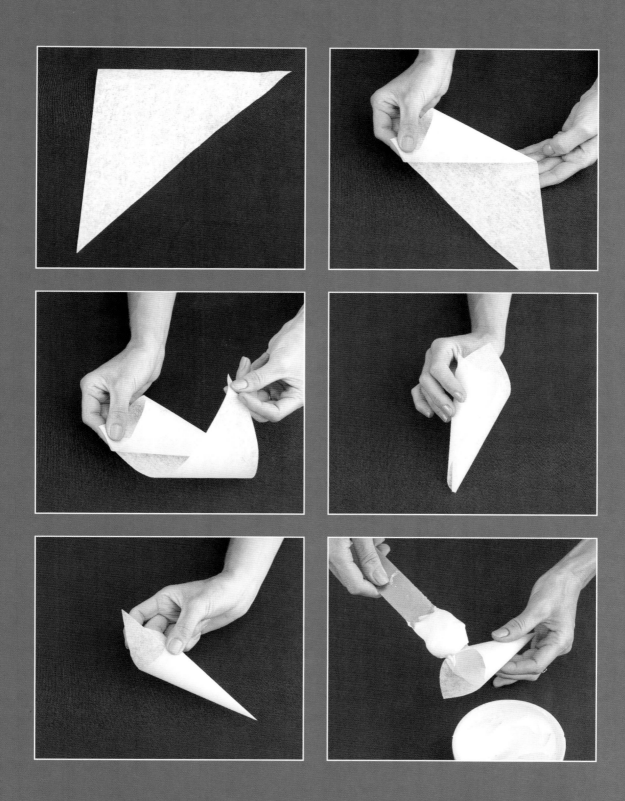

How to Make an Icing Bow

modelling paste (see page 110)
rolled fondant
food colouring paste (optional)
cornflour
water

Mix together the modelling paste and rolled fondant, and mix in food colouring paste if desired.

Dust your work surface and rolling pin with cornflour. Roll out the paste to a thickness of 3mm. Cut the paste into rectangles about 10cm x 15cm. Brush with a little water and fold them in half to form the two loops of the bow.

Stand the loops up on the open end and pinch the ends together to form a pleat. Open out the loop and tuck in the bottom to form a stable base. If the loops are falling in, fill out with some tissue paper. Allow to dry overnight.

To make the bow centre, roll out some more paste to the same thickness. Cut one small rectangle about 5cm x 8cm. Put the two loops close together and wrap the small rectangle around the two loops. Squash the bow centre together underneath the loops.

Cut two long strips about 20cm x 2cm and arrange these under the bow on the cake to form ribbons. Cut a triangle from the bottom of each ribbon. Leave to dry on the cake.

Chocolate Cut-outs

250g dark chocolate, at least
  72% cocoa
chocolate transfer sheet
off-set palette knife
small cutter

Melt the chocolate over a pan of simmering water or in the microwave on Low.
Stir until smooth.

Spread the melted chocolate over a piece of chocolate transfer sheet with a palette knife.
Allow to semi-set, so the chocolate is not brittle, then use a round cutter to cut out disks.
Gently peel the disks away from the sheet, and set aside to set completely.

Caramelised Nuts

350g caster sugar

2 cups slivered almonds or
   whole hazelnuts

Place ½ cup of the sugar into a medium-sized saucepan. Place over a low heat and allow the sugar to begin to dissolve. Gradually add the remaining sugar, stirring gently to combine after each addition. Be careful to ensure the sugar around the edge of the pan doesn't darken and burn.

Once all the sugar has dissolved and the mixture is a golden amber colour, gently stir in the nuts. Working quickly, make sure all the nuts are sugar coated before tipping the mixture onto a piece of baking paper. Gently pull the nuts apart to form small clumps.

Allow to cool until the caramel has set completely before storing in an airtight container for up to 7 days.

Weights and Measures

ABBREVIATIONS

g	gram
kg	kilogram
mm	millimetre
cm	centimetre
ml	millilitre
°C	degrees Celsius

CAKE TIN SIZES

Metric	Imperial/US
15cm	6 inches
18cm	7 inches
20cm	8 inches
23cm	9 inches
25cm	10 inches
28cm	11 inches

WEIGHT CONVERSIONS

Metric	Imperial/US
25g	1 oz
50g	2 oz
75g	3 oz
100g	3½ oz
125g	4½ oz
150g	5 oz
175g	6 oz
200g	7 oz
225g	8 oz
250g	9 oz
275g	9½ oz
300g	10½ oz
325g	11½ oz
350g	12½ oz
375g	13 oz
400g	14 oz
450g	16 oz (1 lb)
500g	17½ oz
750g	26½ oz
1kg	35 oz (2¼ lb)

LENGTH CONVERSIONS

Metric	Imperial/US
0.5cm (5mm)	¼ inch
1cm	½ inch
2.5cm	1 inch
5cm	2 inches
10cm	4 inches
20cm	8 inches
30cm	12 inches (1 foot)

TEMPERATURE CONVERSIONS

Celsius	Fahrenheit	Gas
100°C	225°F	¼
125°C	250°F	½
150°C	300°F	2
160°C	325°F	3
170°C	325°F	3
180°C	350°F	4
190°C	375°F	5
200°C	400°F	6
210°C	425°F	7
220°C	425°F	7
230°C	450°F	8
250°C	500°F	9

LIQUID CONVERSIONS

Metric	Imperial	Cup measures
5ml	¼ fl oz	1 teaspoon
15ml	½ fl oz	1 tablespoon
30ml	1 fl oz	⅛ cup
60ml	2 fl oz	¼ cup
125ml	4 fl oz	½ cup
150ml	5 fl oz (¼ pint)	⅔ cup
175ml	6 fl oz	¾ cup
250ml	8 fl oz	1 cup
300ml	10 fl oz (½ pint)	1¼ cups
375ml	12 fl oz	1½ cups
500ml	16 fl oz	2 cups
600ml	20 fl oz (1 pint)	2½ cups

Note: the Australian metric tablespoon measures 20ml

Index

Acknowledgements

Once again I have people to thank who make the magic of my books happen.

The teams at Graze, Totara Lodge, Tempt and Smith the Grocer who became wholeheartedly involved in the tasting and critiquing of each recipe. It was so important to make sure that each recipe worked, tasted good and that all cake eaters (including non-gluten-free or vegan ones) enjoyed the end result. Your honesty has been much appreciated.

To our fabulous and loyal Tempt customers, who have enjoyed the addition of the new varieties to our shop and now ask for the 'special' cakes more and more.

Thanks must go again to the lovely Christine at New Holland Publishers, who encourages me to think about new projects all the time and gets as excited as me about the end result.

To New Holland Publishers, who gave me a chance with book one and continue to support my endeavours as an author.

Cheers to our new photographer, Devin, for taking the time to come to Wellington and capturing lots and lots of baking in such a beautiful way. I had a great time working with you on this project.

My greatest fans and strongest supporters are my family, both here in New Zealand and in Melbourne. You give me the courage to keep striving to have a go, take on challenges and believe that cake is a breakfast food, too. Sorry to Maddie, Dani and Max that you had to try lots of cakes that were a bit unusual this time, and not a frosting bowl in sight to lick.

And finally to Adam. Once again I couldn't do it without you, your guidance and your love.